Attack Cholesterol

THE DOCTORS' PLAN TO

Attack
Cholesterol

•

ELIZABETH SOMER, MA, RD
AND THE HEALTH MEDIA
EDITORIAL PANEL

foulsham
LONDON • NEW YORK • TORONTO • SYDNEY

foulsham
Yeovil Road, Slough, Berkshire SL1 4JH

ISBN 0–572–01797–9

Copyright © Slawson Communications Inc. 1993

This British Edition © W. Foulsham & Co Ltd

All rights reserved.

The author, editor or publisher cannot assume any
medical or legal responsibility for use of any information
contained herein; this book discusses a wide range of
situations that may not apply in individual cases.

Printed in Great Britain by
St Edmundsbury Press Ltd, Bury St Edmunds, Suffolk

Contents

Introduction

Cholesterol is a type of fat found in food and manufactured in the body. It is an important substance needed for numerous body functions such as nerve transmission, the production of vitamin D and several hormones that regulate the body processes, and the formation of bile that aids in the digestion of foods.

Excess cholesterol in the blood, however, might increase a person's risk of developing cardiovascular disease (CVD), which is a leading cause of death. Low to moderate levels of cholesterol in the blood are associated with a reduced risk of developing CVD. The maintenance of healthy blood levels of cholesterol might be influenced by good nutrition.

ATTACK CHOLESTEROL will help your understanding of cholesterol, the process of atherosclerosis, the relationship between cholesterol and cardiovascular disease, and how to design a nutritious diet that might prevent or treat diseases of the heart and blood vessels.

1
Cholesterol And Cardiovascular Disease (CVD)

Our parents or grandparents died from infectious diseases such as tuberculosis, smallpox, and pneumonia. These diseases have now been almost eliminated with the development of sanitation measures, of effective vaccines, and mass immunisation.

While the death rate from the major infectious diseases dropped after 1910, the death rate from chronic degenerative diseases increased more than 250%. Chronic degenerative diseases include cardiovascular (heart and blood vessel) disease (CVD), cancer, diabetes, and hypertension.

Today, cardiovascular disease accounts for 50% of all death in the United States; cancer accounts for another 20%. These diseases are primarily a result of lifestyle and might be slowed or halted if every person adopts healthy habits. (*Figure 1, overleaf*)

Who Is At Risk Of Developing Cardiovascular Disease?

"A man is only as old as his arteries."
Sir William Osler, M.D.

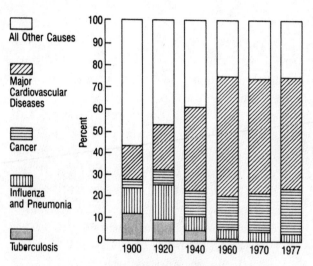

Source: National Center for Health Statistics, Division of Vital Statistics

Figure 1.

Deaths for Selected Causes as a Percent of all Deaths: United States, Selected Years, 1900–1977.

Of the deaths caused by degenerative diseases, 50% are due to unhealthy behaviours, 20% are due to environmental factors, 20% are due to biological factors and only 10% are due to inadequacies in the health care system.

Several risk factors will encourage the development of CVD. They are classified into primary and secondary risk factors, depending on the strength of their influence. The three primary risk factors for CVD are:

1. **Hypertension:** The World Health Organisation has stated that a blood pressure reading greater than 160/95 indicates hypertension. A well-known heart study, however, shows a risk at almost any level.

2. **Cigarette smoking:** The risk of death from CVD is twice as great among smokers as non-smokers. Smokers who periodically discontinue smoking have a risk level between those who smoke and those who do not smoke. Smoking should be discontinued.

3. **Elevated blood cholesterol:** As blood cholesterol levels rise above 150 mg/dl

of blood, so does a person's risk for CVD.

Since these three factors were identified, a fourth primary risk factor has been added:

4. **Elevated LDL-cholesterol**.

Secondary risk factors for the development of CVD include:

1. Obesity (a body weight, as fat, that is 15% to 20% above ideal)
2. Diabetes
3. Stress
4. Lack of exercise
5. A family history of CVD
6. Male gender
7. Stress-prone personality
8. High blood triglycerides
9. Increasing age.

If an individual has three or more of the primary or secondary risk factors, the chance of developing CVD is six times greater than if only one risk factor is present.

Atherosclerosis: The Beginning of Cardiovascular Disease

The primary cause of heart and blood vessel disease is atherosclerosis. Atherosclerosis is a form of arteriosclerosis or "hardening of the arteries." This is a progressive accumulation of cholesterol in the arteries and the degeneration of the arteries. The artery walls gradually thicken with cholesterol "plaque" and the diameter of the artery narrows. This reduces the amount of oxygen-carrying blood that can reach the heart, brain or other organs. (*Figure 2, Page 16*)

Coronary heart disease is a restriction of blood, nutrients and oxygen to the heart. Angina pectoris, or chest pain, is a symptom of this disorder. If blood flow is blocked completely, the result is heart attack and possibly death.

Damage to the arteries that feed the brain results in cerebrovascular disease or a stroke. Strokes also can result from a damaged artery that ruptures. The severity of the stroke depends on how much tissue is deprived of blood and the length of time it is deprived of blood.

The normal elasticity of a healthy artery

The Progression Of Atherosclerosis

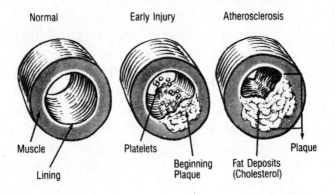

Normal   Early Injury   Atherosclerosis

Muscle   Platelets   Plaque

Lining   Beginning Plaque   Fat Deposits (Cholesterol)

Figure 2.

The underlying cause of heart and blood vessel disease is atherosclerosis. This is a progressive accumulation of cholesterol in the arteries and degeneration of the arteries that reduces the amount of oxygen-carrying blood to the heart, brain or other organs.

allows it both to expand and to contract to regulate blood pressure. This elasticity decreases in the atherosclerotic artery as it engorges with cholesterol and becomes rigid. Without internal control to regulate blood pressure, hypertension (high blood pressure) can result.

Blood clots are more likely to develop around fat-clogged arteries. These blood clots further restrict blood flow and, if dislodged, can travel to other arteries obstructed by atherosclerotic plaque. These blood clots are often the cause of sudden heart attack or stroke.

The causes of atherosclerosis are poorly understood. The damage might be caused by the following:

- a virus
- carbon monoxide from cigarette smoke
- hypertension
- substances in the blood that initiate the damage.

The common thread that connects almost every theory of atherogenesis, the start of atherosclerosis, is cholesterol. Three important points are worth noting:

1. As blood fats increase (especially cholesterol) so does the risk for atherosclerosis.
2. Anything that lowers blood cholesterol lowers the risk for cardiovascular disease.

3. Dietary cholesterol and saturated fats increase the level of cholesterol in the blood and removal from the diet lowers it.

Blood Cholesterol And Atherosclerosis

A person's blood cholesterol level is unequivocally linked to subsequent risk of CVD.

Three major studies support this link between cholesterol and the risk of developing cardiovascular disease:

1. The Seven Countries Study investigated heart disease rates in populations from Italy to New York.
2. The Ni-Hon-San Study studied heart disease rates in populations as they migrated from Japan to Hawaii and finally to San Francisco.
3. The Framingham Heart Study collected information for 20 years on a population living in Framingham, Massachusetts.

All three studies showed that blood cholesterol levels are the greatest indicator of subsequent risk for cardiovascular disease. The Framingham Heart Study also showed that as blood cholesterol rose from 150 mg%* to 260 mg%, the risk of heart disease tripled. Countries where people have high blood cholesterol levels also have populations with the highest incidence of heart attacks and deaths from CVD. Countries where people have relatively low blood cholesterol levels have populations with little or no cardiovascular disease.

The Role Of Lipoproteins In Cardiovascular Disease

Cholesterol cannot float freely in the watery medium of the blood; therefore, the body packages all fats, including cholesterol, in carriers called lipoproteins. These carriers contain a water-soluble outer layer with an inner core of cholesterol and other fats. (*See page 39 for a further discussion of lipoproteins and the fats they carry.*) Some lipoproteins are associated with an

---

*Cholesterol is measured in the blood as milligrams of cholesterol per decilitre of blood (mg/dl) which can be simplified to mg%.

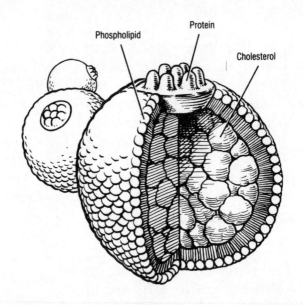

Figure 3. A Lipoprotein

Cholesterol is packaged in lipoproteins so they can be transported in the blood. These lipoproteins are covered in a water-soluble layer of protein and phospholipids and have an inner core where the fat-soluble cholesterol and triglycerides are carried.

increased risk of developing CVD while others have a protective effect. (*Figure 3*)

The Framingham Heart Study showed that when a large proportion of cholesterol

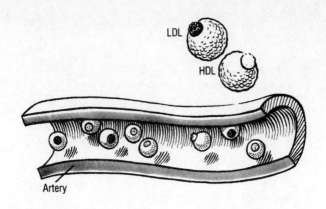

Figure 4. Longitudinal Section of Artery with HDLs & LDLs

When a large proportion of cholesterol is carried in the high density lipoprotein (HDL-cholesterol) a person is less likely to suffer a premature heart attack.

is carried in the low density lipoproteins (LDLs), a person is more likely to develop atherosclerosis and cardiovascular disease. In contrast, the more cholesterol that is carried in the high density lipoproteins (HDLs) the less likely a person is to suffer a heart attack. (*Figure 4*) Current research suggests that measuring HDL- and LDL-cholesterol is a more accurate indicator of cardiovascular disease risk than measuring total blood cholesterol. These values can vary as a result of several lifestyle and biological factors:

LDL increases with: age, obesity, lack of exercise, cigarette smoking, a high fat and cholesterol diet.

HDL increases with: maintenance of ideal body weight, regular and vigorous aerobic exercise, a low-fat and low cholesterol diet, non-smoking, and moderate alcohol consumption.

HDL decreases with: oral contraceptive pills, obesity and smoking.

Blood Cholesterol Levels: "Normal" Versus Optimal

Blood cholesterol levels are one of the best indicators of whether a person will develop cardiovascular disease. When a blood test report states that blood cholesterol is "normal", an individual might assume that the risk of developing heart disease is low. This might not be true.

"Normal" values in the United States are between 220 mg% and 260 mg%. These are not "normal." They are average values for a population where one in every two persons will die from heart or blood vessel disease.

There is controversy about what is the best level for blood cholesterol. A conservative estimate shows that the best level is somewhere below 200 mg%. In a recent report published by the American Heart Association this level was designated as a range between 130 mg% and 190 mg%. More than half of the adult men in the United States have blood cholesterol levels greater than 200 mg%. A third of the males between the ages of 34-years-old and 44-years have hypercholesterolemia (i.e. high blood cholesterol) with values equal to or exceeding 260 mg%. Although a reduction in cholesterol level is thus important, evidence suggests that very low cholesterol levels might be linked to the risk of developing cancer.

How can a person determine his or her risk of cardiovascular disease? The medical director of the Framingham Heart Study has recommended a value not only for total blood cholesterol, but even more importantly, for the ratio between total cholesterol and HDL-cholesterol. The following three steps should be taken to identify your personal risk of developing cardiovascular disease.

1. Have a blood test to determine total cholesterol and HDL-cholesterol. The latter value is not always included in a cholesterol test and must be requested.
2. Do not accept a diagnosis of "normal." Ask to see the value for both measurements. If the value for total cholesterol is 150 mg% or below the risk for CVD is low. A person should check his or her cholesterol level perodically (not less than once a year after the age of 35) to stay within the safe zone.
3. If total cholesterol is above 150 mg%, the ratio of total cholesterol to HDL-cholesterol should be assessed. This can be done by dividing the total cholesterol figure by the HDL-cholesterol. If the ratio is below 4.5:1, the risk for cardiovascular disease is moderate. If the ratio is below 3.5:1 the risk is low. Monitor total cholesterol and HDL-cholesterol periodically to make sure it does not fall into the danger zone. If the ratio is greater than 4.5:1, a person may be at risk of developing premature cardiovascular disease. (*Table 1, Page 25*)

Table 1	Determining Total Cholesterol To HDL-Cholesterol Ratio

$$\frac{\text{Total Cholesterol (mg/dl of blood)}}{\text{HDL-Cholesterol (mg/dl of blood)}} =$$

Example A:

$$\frac{260 \text{ mg/dl Total Cholesterol}}{40 \text{ mg/dl HDL-Cholesterol}} = 6.5{:}1^*$$

*This person is at high risk for suffering premature atherosclerosis, heart disease, or stroke before age 60.

Example B:

$$\frac{200 \text{ mg/dl Total Cholesterol}}{60 \text{ mg/dl HDL-Cholesterol}} = 3.0{:}1^{**}$$

**This person is at low risk for atherosclerosis, heart disease, or stroke.

Cholesterol And Cardiovascular Disease: In Summary

More people will die from heart or blood vessel diseases this year than from all other diseases, except cancer and accidents combined. CVD is a silent killer; more than 25% of CVD victims suffer a fatal heart attack without any prior symptoms. If a person is fortunate, he or she will develop a warning sign such as angina (chest pain). This often occurs, however, in the later stages of the disease.

The belief that CVD develops in the middle to later years is false. Cholesterol is deposited into the arteries of the heart or brain at a rate of 1% to 2% each year from childhood. It is only in the middle to later years, however, that the arteries are so obstructed that blood flow is severely reduced or blocked.

There is something each individual can do to decrease the risk of developing CVD. A simple blood test for total cholesterol and HDL-cholesterol is the best indicator of the risk for developing premature heart and blood vessel disease. *If total cholesterol is above 150 mg% or the ratio of total cholesterol to HDL-cholesterol is above 4.5:1, action should be taken to reduce the level of cholesterol in the blood.*

Medications And Cholesterol

Medication is effective in the reduction of cholesterol and in the relief of some heart disease symptoms such as angina. Unfortunately, almost all drugs have side effects, some of which increase a person's risk for developing CVD. In addition, most drugs are designed for the treatment of disease; they are seldom used for prevention.

Some drugs lower total cholesterol levels and might also increase HDL-cholesterol. Medications such as clofibrate, colestipol, and cholestyramine increase the excretion of cholesterol and bile or alter the body's production or use of cholesterol. The side effects of these drugs range from angina, steatorrhea (fatty stool), arrhythmia, and gall stones to deficiencies in the fat-soluble vitamins A, D, E and K.

Other medications, called beta blockers, reduce the heart's demand for oxygen and alleviate angina and the other symptoms of diseased coronary arteries. These medications might produce fatigue, depression, impotence, and might also elevate total cholesterol and lower HDL-cholesterol.

The benefits of taking these medications, however, outweigh the possibility of experiencing adverse side effects. It is also important to emphasise the effect of a nutritious diet in the prevention and treatment of heart disease. This approach does not have adverse side effects.

2
Cholesterol: The Basics

What Is Cholesterol?

Cholesterol is a type of fat. Some fats are easy to recognise because they are visible as the marbling in meat or the butter on toast, but 60% of the fat consumed in the diet is invisible. It is hidden in the lean portion of meats, egg yolks, nuts, or other foods. Cholesterol cannot be seen in foods and that is why it is widely considered an "invisible" fat.

Cholesterol is found in limited supply in the body and the diet when compared to other fats. About 95% of the fats in foods and in the body are triglycerides. Triglycerides are commonly known as saturated or unsaturated fats. Saturated fats are primarily found in foods that come from animal sources such as butter, meats, offal, and whole milk. Unsaturated fats are found in oils, whole grains, avocados, and other vegetable foods. Triglycerides, not cholesterol, are the fats that supply calories (9 calories/gram), accumulate around the waist, and give food its aroma and tenderness.

The structure of cholesterol is different from other fats. Cholesterol has a round shape in contrast to the linear, three-tailed structure of triglycerides. (*Figure 5*)

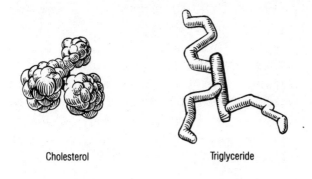

Cholesterol   Triglyceride

Figure 5. Structure of Cholesterol

The chemical structure of cholesterol is different from other fats. Cholesterol has a fat, ring structure in contrast to the thin, three-tailed structure of triglycerides.

What Does Cholesterol Do?

Cholesterol is controversial because of its association with cardiovascular disease, but the 60 to 150 grams of cholesterol in the body perform several important functions.

Maintenance Of Healthy Brain And Nerve Tissue

Cholesterol is present in every cell in the body and is a part of all cell membranes. As much as 50% of the insulation cover (the myelin sheath) around nerve cells is composed of cholesterol. This sheath assists with normal nerve conduction and transmission. Without this well-developed insulation nerves could not fire properly, which would result in such nerve dysfunctions as poor coordination and speech impairment.

Formation Of Vitamin D And The Steroid Hormones

Cholesterol is a building block for numerous substances in the body.

Vitamin D is produced in the skin from cholesterol and sunlight. For this reason, the skin stores cholesterol. Endocrine glands such as the adrenals, ovaries, and testes store cholesterol for conversion to the hormones: oestrogen, progesterone, testosterone, cortisone, cortisol, and aldosterone. This group of hormones is called the "steroid" hormones because they are formed from cholesterol, which is a type of fat called a sterol. These hormones participate in thousands of body functions from the development and maintenance of sex characteristics to carbohydrate and protein metabolism.

Production Of Bile

Cholesterol is a building block of bile. Bile aids in the digestion and absorption of fats and the fat-soluble vitamins.

The liver converts cholesterol to bile. Bile assists with fat absorption. Bile is stored in the gall bladder and is released into the small intestine after each meal is consumed.

Bile breaks fats apart in the small intestines. This action is like adding a substance to oil and vinegar salad dressing so that the oil will stay suspended in the vinegar solution. In the intestines, bile breaks fat globules into thousands of tiny droplets, so digestive substances can divide these droplets into smaller particles for absorption. (*Figure 6, Page 33*)

Anything that interferes with either the production or release of bile results in excessive accumulation of undigested fat in the intestines and a condition called steatorrhea (fatty stools). A person with this condition cannot absorb sufficient calories to maintain normal weight and will lose muscle tissue and develop symptoms of vitamin deficiencies. Bile is essential for the absorption of dietary fats, including the fat-soluble vitamins, and the maintenance of normal body weight and health.

Another condition related to cholesterol is gallstones. While bile is stored in the gall bladder, its cholesterol can crystallise. These crystals are the stones that cause abdominal pain and have to be removed. High levels of cholesterol in the blood are associated with an increased risk of developing gallstones.

Bile is the final product of cholesterol metabolism. Bile is the primary means by

Emulsification of Fats by Bile

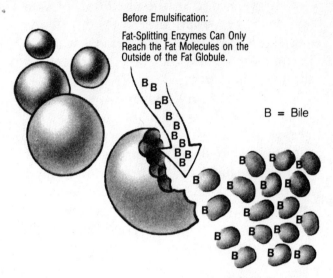

Before Emulsification:

Fat-Splitting Enzymes Can Only Reach the Fat Molecules on the Outside of the Fat Globule.

B = Bile

After Emulsification:

Fat-Splitting Enzymes Can Make Physical Contact With Fat Molecules.

Figure 6.

Bile acts like an emulsifer in the small intestine to break down large fat globules into tiny droplets. This increases the surface area of the fat and aids in digestion.

which the body rids itself of excess cholesterol. Minute amounts of cholesterol are
lost in sweat and in the shedding of skin
and hair. However, over 80% of all the
cholesterol not used in the body, whether
it comes from the diet or is produced by
the liver, is converted to bile.

The body is very efficient in conserving
bile. As much as 90% of the 20 to 30
grams of bile excreted each day into the
intestines is reabsorbed through the lining
of the intestine and returned to the liver
to be reused. Any dietary substance or
medication that inhibits this reabsorption
decreases the amount of cholesterol in the
body and in the blood.

Where Does Cholesterol Come From?

Cholesterol in the body comes from two
sources: from the diet and from the liver,
where it is manufactured.

Dietary cholesterol is not an essential
nutrient. If an individual never ingested
another milligram, body processes would
continue to function. The liver manufac-
tures about 2,000 milligrams of cholesterol

each day, which is more than the 500 to 750 milligrams the average individual eats each day.

To maintain a balance, a mechanism exists between our dietary intake and the production of cholesterol in the liver. In healthy individuals this mechanism keeps the level of cholesterol within a safe and adequate range. In some individuals, especially those who consume large amounts of dietary cholesterol, this mechanism either fails to work effectively or stops working because of the overload. Under these conditions, cholesterol levels in the blood can rise.

Dietary Sources Of Cholesterol

A vegetable oil advertised as "Cholesterol Free" is no different from any other vegetable oil on the supermarket shelf. All vegetable oils are cholesterol-free. Only foods from animal sources, not vegetable sources, contain cholesterol.

Leading medical experts in the fields of nutrition and heart disease have advised that an individual restrict cholesterol intake to less than 300 mg each day; and yet many people take in at least 500 mg each day. Egg yolks are the most concentrated source of cholesterol, with each yolk providing between 250 and 300 mg; egg whites do not contain cholesterol. Offal, such as liver, kidney, and heart, contain large concentrations of cholesterol. Red meats are a major source of cholesterol.

The dark meat of both chicken and turkey contains more cholesterol than the white meat. Removing the skin before cooking will eliminate a lot of the fat. Other sources of cholesterol include beef, pork, lamb, luncheon meats, hot dogs, and shellfish. Fish and poultry without the skin have small amounts of cholesterol.

The butterfat in dairy foods contains cholesterol. In general, the greater the fat content of the dairy food, the greater the cholesterol content. Whole milk contains more cholesterol than low-fat milk and non-fat milk contains very little cholesterol. Any dairy food mixed with egg yolks, such as custard, ice cream, or rich milk pudding, is high in cholesterol.

Grain foods that contain cholesterol include waffles, pancakes, muffins, cake, and noodles. The cholesterol content in

Table 2   Cholesterol, Saturated Fat and Fat Content of Selected Foods

	Cholesterol (mg)	Total Fat (g)	Total Saturated Fat (g)
Bacon, 2 slices	10.0	5.2	1.7
Beef, 3 oz./80g*	77.0	7.5	3.6
Butter, 1 teaspoon or pat	11.7	4.1	2.2
Cheddar cheese, 1 oz./25g	28.0	9.1	5.0
Chicken, light meat, 3 oz./80g	66.9	5.3	1.5
Cream, heavy, 1 tbsp.	20.0	5.6	3.1
Egg, 1 large	252.0	5.8	1.8
Ice cream, 8 oz./225g	53.0	14.1	7.8
Lamb, 3 oz./80g	85.0	7.0	3.9
Margarine 1 teaspoon or pat	0	3.8	2.7
Milk, 8 fl.oz. whole, 3.5% fat	34.0	8.5	4.7
Milk, 8 fl.oz. low fat, 2% fat	22.0	4.9	2.7
Pork, 3 oz./80g	75.0	10.0	3.6
Salad dressing, French 1 tbsp.	0	6.2	1.1
Salmon, tinned, 4 oz./110g	39.8	15.9	4.9
Shrimp, 3 oz./80g	127.5	0.9	NA**
Yogurt, whole milk, 8 fl.oz.	29.3	8.3	4.6

*Beef, lamb, pork, and veal portions are cooked lean meats and trimmed of separate fat.
**Values not available.

these foods comes from the eggs added during processing. (*Table 2, Page 37*)

Digestion And Absorption Of Cholesterol

The digestion of cholesterol both begins and ends in the small intestine. Bile and substances from the pancreas and from the intestinal lining act on the triglycerides, cholesterol and other dietary fats to break them apart for absorption into the blood or lymph fluid. (*Figure 7*)

The Sources and Functions of Cholesterol

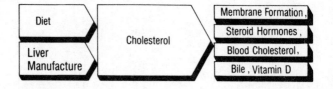

Diet

Liver Manufacture

Cholesterol

Membrane Formation,

Steroid Hormones,

Blood Cholesterol,

Bile, Vitamin D

Figure 7.

The cholesterol that comes from the diet or is manufactured in the liver is used to make vitamin D, bile, and hormones, or is incorporated into every cell membrane.

Transportation Of Cholesterol: Lipoproteins

Cholesterol is transported in the watery fluids of the body (blood and lymph) in lipoproteins. These "carriers" are water-soluble on the outside and fat-soluble on the inside. The water-soluble coating lets cholesterol and other fats move throughout the body without clogging the blood vessels and other tissues. Lipoproteins are spherical in shape and vary in their size, density, and composition. (*Figure 3, Page 20*)

The family of lipoproteins include:

1. chylomincrons
2. very low density lipoproteins (VLDL)
3. low density lipoproteins (LDL)
4. high density lipoproteins (HDL)

The lipoproteins are named according to their degree of density. Those containing the most triglycerides and the least protein are less dense. For instance, VLDLs contain only 9% protein, whereas LDLs contain 21% protein and HDLs contain more than 50% protein.

Chylomicrons contain the least amount of protein, only 2%. These lipoproteins package cholesterol and other fats entering the body from the small intestines and transport them to the tissues.

Very low density lipoproteins (VLDLs) perform a function similar to chylomicrons but instead of transporting incoming fats, they package triglycerides and cholesterol produced within the body and transport them to the body's cells. When VLDLs reach their destination, they release their contents, change their proteins, and are converted to low density lipoproteins (LDLs).

While triglycerides are the primary fat in chylomicrons and VLDLs, the primary fat in the LDLs and HDLs is cholesterol. Approximately three-quarters of all the cholesterol in the blood is packaged in LDLs.

The difference between LDLs and HDLs is their destination. LDLs transport cholesterol from the liver to the body's cells. HDLs scavenge excess cholesterol from the body's cells and carry it back to the liver to be converted to bile. Since the major route of cholesterol excretion is through bile formation, the HDLs reduce the level of cholesterol circulating in the blood.

3

Diet And Cardiovascular Disease

Since the turn of the century our diet has changed significantly, as can be seen from a detailed American survey of eating habits in 1910 and today (*Figure 8, Page 42*). Some of these changes are related to the increase in illness and death from CVD.

1. There has been an increase in our fat consumption. Fat constitutes 42% of our calories today. This is 31% more fat than our parents and grandparents consumed in 1910.
2. There has been a decrease in starch, which is the complex carbohydrates found in cereals, breads, dried beans and peas, and vegetables. Starch accounts for only 21% of the calories in the typical diet. Starch consumption is down 93% since the turn of the century.

Figure 8. American Diet Since 1910

1910

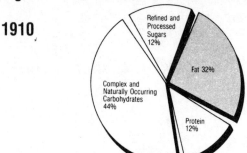

Current American Diet

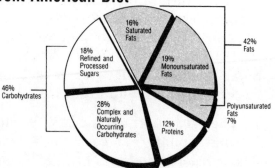

Goal

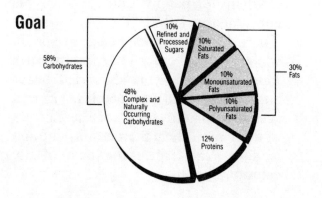

3. There has been an increase in sugar consumption. Refined sugar, corn syrup, and other sweeteners account for 18% of our calories, 50% more than in 1910.

These changes are linked to important changes in our health. The new diet, in combination with a sedentary lifestyle, has contributed to an epidemic of obesity, diabetes, cardiovascular disease, stroke and some forms of cancer.

Does Diet Influence Blood Cholesterol?

Elevated cholesterol is linked to an increased risk of developing atherosclerosis and other cardiovascular diseases. Recently an important link was added to the chain linking diet to cholesterol and cholesterol to CVD.

In general, the more fat and cholesterol in the diet, the higher the blood cholesterol levels and the greater the incidence of cardiovascular disease.

In the Seven Countries Study and the Ni-Hon-San Study dietary intake of fat corresponded with blood cholesterol levels and risk for heart disease. In the latter study, as the Japanese subjects migrated from their native homeland to Hawaii and finally to California, both their fat and cholesterol intake increased, their blood cholesterol rose, and their incidence of cardiovascular disease rose. The Chicago Western Electric Study studied 1,900 middle-aged men over a 19 year period to find a dietary link with heart disease. Again, as their dietary fat increased, so did blood cholesterol levels.

Although some studies have not found a relationship between intake of dietary fat and cholesterol, the evidence from well-designed studies supports the diet-heart connection; dietary fats are linked to levels of cholesterol in the blood. However, not all fats are alike. Some dietary fats raise blood cholesterol and others lower blood cholesterol.

Saturated Fats, Cholesterol, And Cardiovascular Disease

The two dietary fats linked to an increased risk of heart disease are the saturated fats and cholesterol.

A diet primarily composed of red meats, whole milk and other fatty dairy foods, and foods fried or sauteed in butter, shortening, or margarine will elevate blood cholesterol and LDL-cholesterol levels. The way in which these saturated fats raise blood cholesterol is not understood. Saturated fats in the diet might increase dietary absorption of cholesterol or liver manufacture of cholesterol. Excesses of these fats might alter other blood factors, such as prostaglandins and platelets that are important in the initiation and progression of atherosclerosis.

Since both saturated fats and cholesterol are found in foods from animal sources, it might be a combination of the two that is associated with increased blood cholesterol and risk of cardiovascular disease. Quite apart from saturated fat, however, dietary cholesterol increases blood cholesterol and might place a person at greater risk for having a heart attack.

Olive Oil And Cardiovascular Disease

In the Mediterranean countries, where the diet is high in olive oil, the incidence of cardiovascular disease is low. The primary fat in olive oil is an unsaturated fat called oleic acid. This fat apparently does not increase blood cholesterol levels and it might lower them.

Vegetable Oils And Cardiovascular Disease

When the greater proportion of fat in the diet comes from vegetable oils, the risk for heart disease is low. Vegetable oils might increase intestinal excretion of cholesterol and bile acids. This reduced absorption would contribute to lower levels of cholesterol in the blood.

The polyunsaturated fats in vegetable oils contain linoleic acid, linolenic acid, and arachidonic acid. These fatty acids are the building blocks for the important hormone-like substances in blood called prostaglandins that assist in the regulation of blood pressure and wound healing.

High blood levels of some prostaglandins might indicate atherosclerosis while other prostaglandins might protect against the disease. These prostaglandins can be somewhat controlled through diet.

Vegetable Oils, Platelets, Prostaglandins, And Cardiovascular Disease

When an artery wall is damaged, many processes start to mend the damage. Platelets, which are cell fragments important in blood clotting and wound healing, are attracted to the damaged artery. In healthy individuals, platelets stop excessive bleeding and assist in the normal repair process. In atherosclerosis, however, these same cell fragments are linked to further progression of the disease.

Once platelets have gathered at the injured site, they release a prostaglandin called thromboxane. Thromboxane causes the artery wall to constrict and spasm, and stimulates additional clustering of platelets at the damaged area. Both of these two actions cause injury to the artery wall and possible progression of atherosclerosis. A cycle is then established. Platelets produce more thromboxane that causes further damage and attracts more platelets. This chronic irritation to the artery wall might be aggravated by cholesterol being deposited into the wound. It is one of the ways atherosclerosis might begin. This theory is supported by reports that people with CVD have higher circulating levels of platelets and thromboxane than people who do not have the disease. (*Figure 9, opposite*)

In contrast, the artery walls produce another prostaglandin called prostacyclin. Prostacyclin produces the opposite effect of thromboxane. It inhibits the clumping of platelets at the injured site and it relaxes the artery walls.

The dietary fats linoleic and linolenic acids are the building blocks of both thromboxane and prostacyclin. The balance between these two prostaglandins depends on linoleic acid and linolenic acid and on the amount and type of fats in the diet. If the diet is high in polyunsaturated fats and low in the saturated fats, the formation of thromboxane is restricted and the formation of prostacyclin is increased. Platelet clustering and resultant artery wall

A Possible Theory for the Beginning of Atherosclerosis

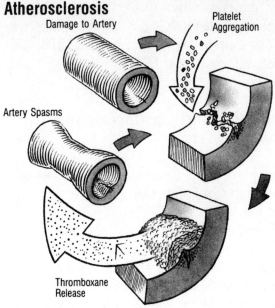

Damage to Artery

Platelet Aggregation

Artery Spasms

Thromboxane Release

Figure 9.

A proposed theory for the initiation of atherosclerosis. The damaged artery attracts blood cell fragments called platelets. These platelets release a substance called thromboxane that causes the artery to spasm, which causes more damage to the artery. A cycle develops that causes more and more damage to the artery, the accumulation of cholesterol, and the development of atherosclerosis.

constriction and spasms may reduce. This may explain why a diet with a higher amount of vegetable oils than animal fats is associated with a reduced risk for atherosclerosis and CVD.

Fish Oils And Cardiovascular Disease

There are few reports of cardiovascular disease in Greenland Eskimos even though they eat a diet rich in fat.

The dietary fat eaten by the Eskimos is made primarily from fish oils, which contain a beneficial fat called eicosapentaenoic acid or EPA. The low blood cholesterol levels of these people is due to their high EPA diet. When EPA is fed to non-Eskimo populations their blood cholesterol profiles immediately improve and remain low even after EPA is removed from the diet. In addition, platelet aggregation is reduced and HDL-cholesterol is increased. Thromboxane levels, LDL-cholesterol levels, triglyceride levels, and blood pressure also decline. (*Table 3, opposite*)

The research on EPA is new. Although EPA seems to reduce both platelet clumping

Table 3	EPA Content of Selected Fish	
Species	Percent of Calories from Fat	EPA (grams per 4 oz/110g)
Cod	8	0.3
Red Snapper	11	0.4
Tuna, white in water	14	0.5
Squid	20	1.0
Rainbow Trout	31	1.2
Herring, Atlantic	43	1.3
Mackerel, Atlantic	52	2.5
Salmon, tinned	57	3.3
Salmon, fresh	59	2.4

All values are for cooked fish.

and also the symptoms of cardiovascular disease, it is premature to make recommendations for its therapeutic use. The only known adverse side effect from the use of EPA supplements is prolonged bleeding time caused by the reduced activity of platelets. A physician should be consulted before EPA supplements are consumed.

Is Diet Related To Cardiovascular Disease?

Diet influences blood cholesterol levels and blood cholesterol influences the risk for CVD, but does diet influence CVD? Here the debate on the diet and cardiovascular disease link becomes heated. This piece in the puzzle will continue to be debated; however, good evidence exists that diet can prevent and treat atherosclerosis and its damage to the arteries and the heart.

Reports published by the Lipid Research Clinics showed that for every 1% reduction in cholesterol there is a 2% reduction in the risk of developing CVD. Researchers used the drug cholestyramine to lower cholesterol levels, but stated that anything that would lower cholesterol would have the same effect. A low fat, low cholesterol, high fibre diet will lower cholesterol levels.

Making changes in lifelong dietary habits can be difficult. If an individual's diet is not altered prior to the development of atherosclerosis and CVD, it will have to be changed at a later date. The primary reason for performing coronary artery bypass surgery is to relieve debilitating angina, to salvage the heart at risk from heart attack and possibly prevent death. Surgery does not halt the progression of atherosclerosis and bypass grafts are more prone to the degenerative disease than the diseased arteries they replace. Unless diet patterns that promoted atherosclerosis are changed, many patients exhibit CVD symptoms again within three to five years.

Regression Of Atherosclerosis

Evidence shows that atherosclerosis might be prevented, its progression might be stopped, and its damage might be reversed to some degree.

Studies show at least partial regression of atherosclerosis treated with drugs or diet. Preliminary results show that as much as 90% of atherosclerosis can be reversed when an individual follows a low fat, low cholesterol, high fibre diet. It is unknown, however, if there is a point where the artery has been permanently damaged from atherosclerosis. It is known that as soon as an individual begins a prudent diet, blood cholesterol levels will usually drop, the atherosclerosis process will be slowed or stopped, and regression is more likely to occur.

4

Dietary Guidelines For A Healthy Heart

The average person consumes the equivalent of 4 oz/110 g of butter in fat and cholesterol each day. Many of us consume far more animal fats than are good for our health.

As long ago as 1977 a United States Senate Select Committee on Nutrition and Human Needs published the US Dietary Goals. These recommendations emphasised the need to reduce dietary fat and cholesterol for the prevention and treatment of CVD. Since that time many experts have repeated the advice that everyone should follow a prudent diet, and have set out similar guidelines. For people with elevated blood cholesterol levels who do not respond to this moderate reduction in fat and cholesterol, a stricter diet is recommended.

The Dietary Goals: A Practical Guide

The Goals for prevention and treatment of CVD extend the recommendations for vitamins and minerals to also include ranges for fat, carbohydrates and sugar. Two servings from the dairy foods are recommended, but the Goals specify that these servings should be low in fat and cholesterol, such as non-fat milk and low-fat cheeses. The protein-rich group is still a daily necessity, but the Goals suggest low-fat selections, such as dried beans and peas, fish and poultry.

Table 4   The US Dietary Goals
1. Maintain ideal body weight.
2. Increase carbohydrate intake to at least 55% of calories consumed.
3. Reduce sugar consumption to below 10% of total calories consumed.
4. Reduce fat intake to no more than 30% of calories consumed.
5. Reduce saturated fat intake to no more than 10% of calories consumed.
6. Reduce daily cholesterol intake to no more than 300 mg.
7. Reduce daily salt intake to less than 5 grams.

The general guidelines for following the US Dietary Goals are as follows:

1. Increase the consumption of whole grain cereals and breads, dried beans and peas, fruits, and vegetables. These foods do not contain cholesterol, have little or no saturated fat, are limited in calories, and provide fibre.
2. Reduce the consumption of refined and processed sugars and foods high in sugars.
3. Reduce the consumption of foods high in fats, especially saturated fats. Consume no more than 6 ounces (160 g) of lean meat or skinned poultry. Increase consumption of fish.
4. Choose low-fat and non-fat dairy foods. The only exception to this goal is infant nutrition.
5. Reduce the consumption of foods high in cholesterol such as butter, egg yolks, fatty meats, and offal.
6. Reduce the consumption of salt and salty foods, especially processed snack foods, canned foods, and convenience foods.

Goal 1: Maintain Ideal Body Weight

Many of us exceed our ideal body weight. Obesity is also linked to the following risk factors for CVD:

- increased levels of blood fats, including cholesterol;
- abnormal levels of lipoproteins in the blood;
- high blood sugar levels and a predisposition to diabetes and heart disease;
- high blood pressure.

A reduction in weight is often associated with a decline in blood fats, and especially cholesterol. For people with CVD, weight at or 10% below ideal weight should be maintained.

Although the Goals focus on diet and nutrition, exercise is a critical component of any weight loss/weight maintenance programme. Weight loss programmes that rely only on caloric restriction might increase the likelihood of malnutrition.

In addition to weight loss, physical activity might provide additional protection from cardiovascular disease because exercise does the following:

- increases HDL-cholesterol (the lipo-proteins associated with a reduced risk for cardiovascular disease);
- lowers LDL-cholesterol (lipoproteins associated with an increased risk for cardiovascular disease);
- normalises blood pressure (high blood pressure along with elevated blood cholesterol is a prime risk factor for the development of cardiovascular disease).

Goals 2 and 3: Increase Carbohydrates And Reduce Sugar

Many low-carbohydrate, high-protein diets have labelled starch as "fattening," but this is not true. All carbohydrates, whether the starch in a potato, the natural sugar in a peach, or the granulated sugar added to a breakfast cereal, provide four calories per gram. This is less than half the calories in an equal amount of fat and the same amount of calories as found in protein. Starchy foods, such as oatmeal, pasta, rice and bread, contain no cholesterol and are low in saturated fat. People who consume a high carbohydrate (starch) diet have a lower incidence of cardio-vascular disease.

Starch in its whole grain form is high in fibre, vitamins and trace minerals. Some forms of fibre, such as oat bran, guar gum that is found in the seeds of some plants, and pectin in fruit, reduce cholesterol levels and help reduce a person's risk for developing CVD. Oat bran can be added to salads, sandwich spreads, casseroles, cereals, soups and stews. Wheat bran does not affect cholesterol levels in the blood and reports show it does not protect against cardiovascular disease. (*Table 5, Page 60*)

Pectin, when consumed in its natural and diluted form in fruits and vegetables, lowers cholesterol. However, consuming concentrated uncooked pectin, used for canning jam and jelly, will not lower cholesterol. Raw canning pectin will cause stomach and intestinal upset, bloating, and possibly diarrhoea.

A recommended dietary fibre intake is not established. It is estimated that a diet that contains about 37 grams (1–1½ ounces) of fibre will provide protective roughage without interfering with the

Table 5 A 45 Gram Fibre Menu

	Meal	Amount	Fibre
Breakfast:	All bran type cereal	1½ oz./30 g	7.9
	Banana	1 medium	1.3
	Milk, non-fat	8 fl. oz.	–
	Orange Juice	6 fl. oz.	0.6
	Whole Wheat Bread	2 slices	5.4
	Jelly	1 tsp	–
	Total fibre content:		**15.2g**
Lunch:	Salad: Spinach	6oz./170g	2.2
	Carrots	3oz./80g	0.8
	Lima beans	2oz./50g	1.8
	Tomato	¼	0.5
	Cheese	2oz./50g	–
	Dressing	1–1½ tbsp	–
	Whole Wheat Roll	1	5.4
	Orange	1	3.8
	Total fibre content:		**14.5g**
Snack:	Tangerine	1	1.8
	Rye Crackers	2	1.5
	Total fibre content:		**3.3g**
Dinner:	Salmon	4oz./110g	–
	Baked potato, with skin	1 medium	5.2
	Yogurt dressing	2 tbsp	–
	Broccoli	3oz./80g	3.2
	Dinner salad	6oz./170g	2.0
	Dressing	2 tsp	–
	Total fibre content:		**10.4g**
Snack:	Cream crackers	2	1.3
	Total fibre content:		**1.3g**
	Total fibre content for the day:		**44.7g**

absorption of other nutrients. This amount can be obtained each day from:

- 6 servings of whole grain breads and cereals (1 serving = 1 slice of bread; 3oz./80g cooked pasta, rice, or cereal; or 2oz./50g whole grain cold cereal) ... .13 grams
- 4 servings of fresh fruit and vegetables (1 serving = 1 piece, 4oz./110g fruit or vegetable) ....15–23 grams
- 1 serving of dried beans or peas (1 serving = 3oz./80g) ....9 grams
- Total daily fibre intake ...37–45 grams

Meals should include rice, noodles, cereals, breads, fruits, vegetables, dried beans and peas, and foods from other plant sources for an individual to consume 55% or more of their total calories as starch or complex carbohydrates.

Every year the average American eats his or her weight in sugar. That consumption totals 40 teaspoons a day or 640 calories. Sugar is not directly related to CVD or cholesterol levels. However, the majority of people eat either sugary foods in place of nutritious foods and are malnourished, or they eat sugary foods in addition to their daily allotment of nutritious foods and become obese. Both malnutrition and obesity are associated with high levels of cholesterol in the blood.

Many foods have hidden sugar. These foods include ketchup, baked beans, commercial salad dressings, fruit yogurts, tinned meats, packet soups, cereals and pickles. Soft drinks contain between 7 and 10 teaspoons of sugar per serving. The annual *per capita* intake of sugar exceeds 450 servings. *(Table 6, opposite)*

Read labels to spot added sugar. Watch for its aliases, which are dextrose, corn sweetener, honey, sucrose, "natural" sweeteners, or fructose.

Goals 4, 5 And 6: Reduce Fat, Saturated Fat And Cholesterol

Because fat, especially saturated fat and cholesterol, is related to cardiovascular disease and elevated blood cholesterol, fats and fatty foods should be restricted in the diet.

Fat is the most concentrated source of calories in the diet. A teaspoon of oil (5 grams) provides 45 calories of fat. A hamburger, thought to be a high protein food,

Table 6	Hidden Sugars in Foods	
Food	Amount	Sugar (tsp)
Apricots, canned	4 halves/1 tbsp syrup	3½
Beets, pickled	4oz./110g	2
Ketchup	2 tbsp	1½
Chewing gum	1 stick	½
Instant whip	1 tbsp	23
Fruit cocktail	4 fl.oz.	5
Cream cracker	2	1
Grape juice drink	6 fl.oz.	4
Ice cream	4oz./110g	5–6
Jam	1 tbsp	4
Jelly	3oz./80g	4½
Chocolate milk drink	8 fl.oz.	6
Orange juice, imitation	6 fl.oz.	5½
Peas, sweet, tinned	3oz./80g	1
Salad dressing	1 tbsp	¼–¾
Soft drinks	12 fl.oz.	7–9
Yogurt, fruit	8 fl.oz.	7½
Yogurt, frozen	8 fl.oz.	5

derives as much as 75% of its calories from fat. Bacon is 80% fat calories. Whole milk is 50% fat calories, but nonfat milk contains less than 1% fat calories, while providing an easy alternative.

Cholesterol does not supply the body with calories; it cannot be "run off," "sweated out," or "burned up." It is found only in foods from animal sources, especially egg yolks, red meats, offal and some shellfish. (*See page 37 for additional sources of dietary cholesterol*)

Table 7 Recommended Daily Calories from Fat	
Average Daily Calories Needs	Maximum Calories From Fat
1300–1500	390–450
1600–1800	480–540
1900–2100	570–630
2200–2500	660–750
2600–2800	780–840
2900–3100	870–930
3200–3500	960–1050

The Dietary Goals recommend that the fat content of the diet be reduced and that the ratio of polyunsaturated fats to saturated fats be increased. This can be done by maintaining current consumption levels of vegetable oils and reducing saturated fats by eliminating foods from animal sources, hydrogenated vegetable oils such as margarine and shortening, and processed foods that contain palm or coconut oil. (*Table 8, Page 65; Table 9, Page 66; Table 10, Page 67*)

Table 8 Substitutes for High Fat Snacks	
Instead of . . .	**Substitute . . .**
Potato crisps	Pretzels
Peanuts	Popcorn (unbuttered)
Wheat crackers	Rice cakes
Sausage pizza	Cheese pizza
Croissant	Crumpet or roll with apple spread
Milk, whole	Milk, nonfat or low-fat
Ice cream	Sorbet
Cream of mushroom soup	Tomato soup
Mayonnaise	Low-fat imitation mayonnaise
Tuna, packed in oil	Tuna, packed in water
Frozen vegetables in sauce	Frozen vegetables

The following are suggestions for lower fat consumption:

1. Bake, grill, steam, or poach foods. Do not sauté, fry, or use gravies or sauces in cooking.
2. Cook meats at low temperature to increase fat removal.
3. Skim fat from broth before making gravy or soup stock.
4. Do not bread or flour meats. The coating will absorb excess fat.
5. Use non-stick pans, rather than oil or butter.

Table 9   How to Order Low Fat Meals in Restaurants

1. **Appetisers:** Choose fresh fruit and vegetable juice, or seafood cocktail. Say ''no'' to sour cream, seasoned butter, or cream.

2. **Soups:** Choose consomme, barley, vegetable, rice, or split pea soups. Avoid creamed soups or soups with cheese or egg.

3. **Salads:** A wide variety of salad ingredients are low-fat. These include all vegetables, fruits, turkey, chicken, seafood, lean roast beef, or low-fat cheese. Avoid potato salad, cole slaw, and Waldorf salad unless they are made with a small amount of low-calorie mayonnaise. Use salad dressing sparingly or use lemon, vinegar, or yogurt.

4. **Vegetables:** All vegetables are low in fat unless they have been sauteed, deep fried, battered, or cooked in fat.

5. **Entrees:** All varieties of fish (especially good because of its EPA content), chicken, or lean meat can be chosen. Avoid fatty meats, such as goose, duck, prime cuts of beef and all meats that are sauteed, fried, or cooked in batter or gravy.

6. **Breads and Cereals:** Choose whole grain breads and cereal when available. Avoid commercial crackers as they are high in fat and salt. Avoid croissants, sweetened and buttered rolls. Ask the waiter to remove the butter dish from the table.

7. **Desserts:** Choose jellies, fruit ices, fresh fruit, and fresh fruit meringue.

8. In general, avoid foods that have the following words in their description: creamed, cream sauce, au gratin, in cheese sauce, à la mode, marinated, prime, basted, hollandaise, refried, or crispy.

Table 10 Reading Labels with Fat in Mind
When shopping, check labels for the following words that reveal that fat is added to the food. High fat foods contain more than 3 grams of fat for every 100 Calories.

1. animal fat	10. coconut oil
2. bacon fat	11. cream and cream sauce
3. butter	12. hydrogenated vegetable oil
4. egg and egg yolk solids	13. milk chocolate
5. lard	14. whole-milk solids
6. palm oil	15. cocoa butter
7. shortening	16. olive oil
8. vegetable fat	17. peanut oil
9. coconut	18. mustard seed oil

6. Sauté in defatted chicken stock, rather than in oil or butter.

7. Use low-fat or non-fat milk rather than whole milk or cream in cooking.

8. Use two egg whites for every whole egg in recipes. Discard the yolk.

9. Reduce the oil by one-half in recipes.

10. Use jam or marmalade, preferably low calorie, on toast instead of butter.

Goal 7: Reduce Consumption Of Salt And Salty Foods

Hypertension or high blood pressure is a primary risk factor for developing CVD. It is also a disease itself. Mild hypertension can be improved with diet, maintenance of ideal body weight, and exercise.

Sodium intake is associated with high blood pressure in some people. The body's need for sodium is met with as little as 0.2 grams a day, but the average American diet provides over 15 grams (approximately 3 teaspoons). This intake is excessive. A desire for salt food is acquired and is more related to habit than need. Slowly reducing the intake of sodium will not harm health and might help to prevent hypertension.

Beyond The Dietary Goals: Vitamins, Minerals And Other Food Factors

Numerous food substances in addition to fat are being investigated for their effects in lowering cholesterol and the prevention and treatment of cardiovascular disease.

Vitamins

Vitamin C: A low intake of vitamin C is correlated with an increased risk for cardiovascular disease, thrombosis (blood clots), and elevated blood cholesterol. In some people, vitamin C supplements have reduced elevated blood cholesterol and positively affected the ratio of LDL to HDL-cholesterol.

Vitamin B$_6$: In some people, poor dietary intake of vitamin B$_6$ causes damage to the arteries that resembles atherosclerosis.

Niacin: Therapeutic doses of this B vitamin lower blood cholesterol levels and increase HDL-cholesterol. When niacin and the medication colestipol are taken together an even greater reduction in the cholesterol level is seen.

Vitamin E: This fat-soluble vitamin might reduce both the poor circulation in the legs and the lameness associated with atherosclerosis. Supplementation with vitamin E might reduce platelet clumping and raise HDL-cholesterol. In some studies, however, the vitamin has not shown any beneficial effects for patients with CVD.

Vitamin D: This fat-soluble vitamin might aggravate atherosclerosis when consumed in large amounts with dietary cholesterol. For this reason, and because vitamin D can be toxic if taken in doses above 250 μg, it is wise to consume no more than 100% to 300% of the RDA for vitamin D. The RDA for vitamin D is 7.5 μg–10 μg.

Minerals

Copper: Low levels of copper have been associated with elevated blood cholesterol levels and changes in the heart muscle that resemble heart disease.

Chromium: In some cases, chromium supplements have reduced cholesterol and increased HDL-cholesterol.

Magnesium: A low level of magnesium might cause spasms in coronary arteries, angina, arrhythmia (an irregular heart beat), and heart failure.

Other Food Factors

Saponins: Saponins are plant sterols, just as cholesterol is a sterol found in foods from animal sources. Saponins are found in alfalfa meal and sprouts, peanuts, and dried beans and peas. Saponins reduce cholesterol absorption and increase the excretion of bile, thereby lowering levels of cholesterol.

Garlic: Ajoene, one of several hundred compounds in garlic, reduces platelet clumping and might lower blood cholesterol levels. Daily doses of 8 to 9 cloves might lower blood triglycerides and total cholesterol, and raise HDL-cholesterol in healthy people and people with elevated blood fats. But garlic powders and oils do not appear to be as effective as the original plant.

Protein: A vegetarian diet that supplies most of its protein from plant foods is associated with a reduced risk of developing CVD. A vegetarian diet lowers total cholesterol. Plant proteins change the type and amount of amino acids (the components of protein) in the blood that might influence cholesterol levels. A vegetarian diet is high in fibre and polyunsaturated fats and low in saturated fats.

Beyond The Dietary Goals: Alcohol

Early reports stated that moderate alcohol consumption might increase HDL-cholesterol and have a mild protective effect against CVD. However, recent evidence suggests that alcohol might not raise the type of HDL-cholesterol that is beneficial in the prevention of CVD.

Cholesterol: A Summary

As cholesterol levels increase so does the risk for cardiovascular disease. Although this disease might be the number one cause of disability and death in this country, it might be controlled and perhaps prevented if certain healthy diet and life-style habits are followed. A low-fat, low-cholesterol, high-fibre diet combined with physical activity, moderate consumption of alcohol, maintenance of preferred body weight, effective coping skills, and non smoking will help keep cholesterol levels low and help prevent the development of cardiovascular disease.

5

Changing Habits: Guidelines For Success

Awareness of the relationship between diet and both cholesterol and CVD is not useful unless changes are made. Changing habits is not easy. A few simple steps in planning can help a person avoid some of the mistakes when making dietary changes.

First: Complete a seven day food record of the type and amount of all foods and beverages that are consumed. Do not forget to include oils used in cooking, butter on toast, sour cream on a baked potato, or cream in coffee. (For additional sources of fat, see page 37) *(Table 11, Page 74)*

Second: From this food record, identify dietary sources of fat and cholesterol. Also, identify eating patterns that promote fat consumption, i.e. drinking whole milk instead of low-fat or non-fat milk, large

| Table 11 Daily Food Record | | | |
| Day _____ | | | |
Food or Beverage	Amount	Time	Fat Content

servings of meat, ordering foods with sauces and gravies when eating in restaurants, or choosing prime cuts of meat rather than rump, or tenderloin cuts.

Third: From this list of personal dietary fat sources and habits, identify two to three behaviours that are easy to change and are beneficial to health. If the butter on morning toast would not be missed, start off by deleting the butter or using a low-calorie substitute. When one change is successful, other changes that are more complex or difficult can be added. Work on one to three diet changes at a time. It is easy to become overwhelmed if too many changes are started at the same time.

Fourth: For each diet habit that needs to be changed, decide how the change will be made. For example, if the change is to eat less butter in restaurants, the following suggestions might be helpful:

- Ask the waiter to serve all breads dry.
- Identify which of the local restaurants accommodate special orders.
- Enlist family support and reduce the likelihood of saying "One time won't hurt."
- Bring a substitute for butter from home.

- Eat only in restaurants that do not serve butter with a meal.

List as many solutions as possible and from this list pick those solutions that are realistic and possible to follow. From these solutions develop a plan for making a behaviour change. (*Table 12, opposite*)

In order to be successful, a change must be:

1. realistic
2. specific
3. flexible
4. progressively more challenging

Fifth: The identified changes and the planned solutions must be implemented. Practise the changes every day until the changes become habit. Periodically evaluate areas of success and identify areas that need modification.

Once the easier behaviours have been successfully accomplished, go back to the list, identify one to three more habits and follow the same steps to make those changes. Keep in mind that the original changes must be maintained.

The important element in successful behaviour change is progression. Identify

Table 12   Self Assessment of Fat Intake

Ask yourself the following questions about your fat intake:

1. Are fats used in cooking or baking? If so, what type and how much? Eliminate as many fats as possible and substitute vegetable oils for the rest.

2. Are salad dressings or mayonnaise used in salads or sandwiches? Reduce the amount or use a low-calorie substitute.

3. Is fat added or used in cooking vegetables, meats, grains, stuffings, or fruit? Reduce the amount or eliminate the fat.

4. What kind of milk or cream is used as a beverage and in cooking? Substitute nonfat or low-fat milk.

5. Is margarine or butter spread on toast, bread, potatoes, sandwiches, rolls, potatoes, pie crusts, and other foods? Find an alternative, ie., jam, chives, ricotta cheese, honey, or yogurt or eliminate margarine or butter completely.

6. Do gravies, sauces, or syrups accompany foods? Which of these could be reduced or eliminated? Could satisfactory substitutions be found?

7. What ingredients are used in mixed dishes, ie., casseroles, sandwiches, soups, and stews?

8. What cuts of meat are chosen? Is the fat trimmed? Substitute leaner cuts of meat, consume red meats less often, and reduce the portion size to 3 to 4 ounces (80g–110g).

9. What types of cheese are eaten? Choose low-fat cheeses.

10. Are eggs an ingredient in baked goods, ie., biscuits, cakes, custards, croissants, pancakes, or tarts? Use two egg whites for every whole egg and throw the yolk away.

11. Are processed snack foods consumed such as potato crisps, doughnuts, roasted peanuts, or tortilla chips? Try nonfat snack foods such as fresh fruit, vegetables, whole grain rolls, or nonfat yogurt.

eating behaviours in need of change and list them according to ease of change and degree of benefit derived from that change. Do not change all behaviours at one time. Choose one to two actions, then design a specific plan of alternate behaviours, and practise those changes until they become routine. Once successful, begin working on a second target for change.

Figure 10.   The Warning Signs of a Heart Attack

1) Uncomfortable pressure, fullness, squeezing, or pain in the centre of the chest that lasts 2 minutes or more;
2) Pain that spreads to shoulders, neck, or arms;
3) Severe pain, dizziness, fainting, sweating, nausea, or shortness of breath also can occur. Sharp, stabbing pains are usually not signs of a heart attack. Keep a list of emergency rescue service numbers next to the telephone. If pain lasts more than 2 minutes call them immediately. If you can reach the hospital faster by car, have someone drive you. Plan in advance the quickest route to the hospital.

Glossary

Ajoene: A substance in garlic thought to reduce the risk for developing cardiovascular disease.

Angina: Chest pain, which occurs after mild to vigorous exercise or excitement, that is caused by reduced blood supply to the heart because of obstruction of the arteries.

Arrhythmia: Irregular heart beat.

Atherogenesis: The beginning of atherosclerosis in the arteries.

Arteriosclerosis: Hardening and thickening of the arteries. This is a general term that includes several disorders of the arteries.

Artery: A blood vessel that supplies blood, oxygen, and nutrients to the body tissues.

Atherosclerosis: A form of arteriosclerosis characterised by the accumulation of fat in the artery walls. The arteries become roughened and narrowed and blood flow is restricted. It is the primary cause of heart attacks and strokes.

Beta Blockers: Drugs used in the treatment of cardiovascular disease that reduce the heart's demand for blood and inhibit the acceleration of the heart beat.

Bile: A fluid secreted by the liver into the intestines that mixes with other secretions to digest fats.

Bile Acids and Salts: Substances produced in the liver and stored in the gall bladder that are required for the digestion of fats in the intestines. Bile acids and salts are two components of bile.

Blood Cholesterol: Cholesterol, derived from either dietary sources or from body production, that is being transported between the liver and the body tissues. Blood cholesterol is packaged and carried in lipoproteins.

Cardiovascular Disease: A disease of the heart and blood vessels usually caused by the accumulation of atherosclerotic plaque.

Cholesterol: A type of fat found in foods from animal sources and produced by the body. Cholesterol is needed for the production of certain hormones and vitamin D; for healthy nerves and healthy cells throughout the body. Excess cholesterol in the blood is linked to an increase for developing cardiovascular disease.

Cholestyramine: A medication used in the treatment of cardiovascular disease. Cholestyramine binds to bile and dietary cholesterol in the intestines and inhibits absorption; it thereby reduces levels of cholesterol.

Chylomicrons: A type of lipoprotein composed of fats surrounded by a thin protein coat. As dietary fats are absorbed they are packaged in chylomicrons for transportation to the liver.

Clofibrate: A medication used in the treatment of cardiovascular disease. It binds to bile and dietary cholesterol in the intestines and thus inhibits absorption; it reduces cholesterol levels.

Colestipol: A medication used in the treatment of cardiovascular disease. It binds to bile and dietary cholesterol in the intestines and thus inhibits absorption; it reduces cholesterol levels.

Coronary Arteries: The two arteries that encircle the heart and provide it with blood, oxygen, and nutrients and remove waste products and carbon dioxide.

Coronary Bypass Graft Surgery (CABG): Open heart surgery where one or more diseased arteries in the heart are removed and replaced with segments of veins obtained from another part of the body.

Coronary Artery Disease: The disease of the coronary arteries. The arteries develop atherosclerosis, become engorged with fat, and are then unable to provide adequate blood supply to the heart.

Diabetes: A disorder in which the body's ability to use sugar is impaired because of inadequate production or utilisation of the hormone insulin.

Eicosapentaenoic Acid (EPA): A polyunsaturated fatty acid found in fish oils and thought to reduce the risk for cardiovascular disease.

Emulsifier: A compound that holds an oily substance in suspension in a watery liquid, e.g. bile.

Endocrine Glands: Ductless glands that secrete hormones into the body. These hormones have profound effects on other organs and tissues, i.e. ovaries, testes, thyroid, pancreas, and adrenal.

Essential Fatty Acid: A fatty acid that cannot be manufactured in the body and must be supplied by the diet. i.e. linoleic acid.

Four Food Group Plan: A general guide for menu planning that recommends a minimum of the following foods: 4 servings of vegetables and fruits, 4 servings of breads and cereals; 2 servings of milk; and 2 servings of meats or legumes.

Glucose Tolerance Factor: A chromium-containing compound that enhances the function of insulin and helps regulate glucose metabolism.

Gout: A disorder in which excessive accumulation of uric acid in the blood and tissues and deposition of urates in joints cause painful arthritic-type inflammation.

Guar Gum: A water-soluble fibre found in some plants.

Haemorrhage: Seepage of blood from blood vessels into surrounding tissues.

High Density Lipoprotein (HDL): A molecule composed of fats and protein that serves as a transport vehicle for fats in the blood. A high level of HDL is associated with a reduced risk of cardio-vascular disease.

Hormone: A chemical substance produced by a group of cells, or an organ called an endocrine gland, that is released into the blood and transported to another organ or tissue, where it then performs a specific action. i.e. insulin, oestrogen, testosterone, adrenalin.

Hypertension: High blood pressure.

Lesions: Damage to any tissue caused by disease or injury.

Linoleic Acid: An essential polyunsaturated fatty acid.

Linolenic Acid: A polyunsaturated fatty acid.

Lipid: Any one of a number of compounds that are soluble in ether and are called fats.

Lipoprotein: A compound lipid containing fats and protein that serves as the carrier of fats in the watery medium of the blood.

Low Density Lipoprotein (LDL): A molecule comprised of fats and protein that serves as a transport vehicle for fats in the blood. A high level of LDL is associated with an increased risk of cardiovascular disease.

Lymph: The fluid in lymphatic vessels and the lymph spaces. A colourless fluid derived from the blood that is filtered through a special series of vessels and nodes to remove debris and cellular waste products. The filtered lymph is returned to the blood.

Metabolism: The sum total of all body processes, whereby a body converts food into tissues, breaks down and repairs tissues, and converts complex substances into simple ones for energy. Basal metabolism is the minimum amount of energy required to maintain the body processes.

Monounsaturated Fat: A type of fat

such as oleic acid, found in olive oil, avocados, and peanuts.

Oleic acid: A monounsaturated fatty acid.

Pectin: A water-soluble fibre found in fruits.

Phospholipids: A fatty substance that has a fat-soluble end and a water-soluble end and that is an essential part of cell membranes.

Plaque: Accumulation of cholesterol and other fats along the lining of artery walls.

Platelets: Cell fragments in the blood that aid in blood coagulation. Excessive accumulation and clumping of platelets is associated with the development of atherosclerosis.

Precursor: A substance used as a building block for another substance. i.e. the fatty acid linoleic acid is the precursor for prostaglandins.

Prostacyclin: A prostaglandin that dilates

blood vessels and is associated with a reduced risk of cardiovascular disease.

Recommended Dietary Allowances: The amounts of nutrients recommended by the Department of Health to meet the needs of healthy groups of people.

Regression: A term used to describe the removal of atherosclerotic plaque from artery walls.

Saponins: A plant sterol associated with reduced cholesterol levels.

Saturated Fat: A type of fatty acid such as stearic acid, found in meat, butter, and other foods of animal origin.

Sodium: A mineral in salt (sodium chloride), which is associated with hypertension.

Steatorrhea: Excessive amount of fat in the stool.

Sterol: One of the three main classes of fats; a fat with a structure similar to that of cholesterol.

Thiazides: Medications used in the treatment of hypertension.

Thrombosis: The formation of a thrombus or blood clot.

Thromboxane: A prostaglandin that constricts artery walls and is associated with an increased risk of cardiovascular disease.

Triglycerides: One of the three main classes of fats; fatty compounds made up of one glycerol and three fatty acid molecules.

Unsaturated Fat: A type of fat that has one or more spots on the fatty acid for the addition of hydrogen.

Very Low Density Lipoproteins (VLDL): A molecule comprised of fats and protein that serves as a transport vehicle for fats in the blood.

Energy and Minerals Checklist – Needs and Sources

Protein
Daily requirement
men	56 grams
women	44 grams

Sources
6oz./160g turkey	55 grams
8fl.oz./1 cup low fat milk	8 grams
1oz./25g cereal + 4fl.oz./ ½ cup semi-skim milk	6 grams
1 slice wholewheat bread	2.5 grams

Calories
Daily requirement
men	2,000 kcal
women	1,500 kcal

NB People taking strenuous physical exercise add up to 1,000 kcal

Sources
6oz./160g grilled steak	350 kcal
6oz./160g roast chicken without skin	24 0kcal
6oz./160g cod or haddock	120 kcal
6oz./160g chips	420 kcal
medium baked potato	150 kcal
1oz./25g slice of bread	70 kcal
1oz./25g butter	225 kcal

1oz./25g cheddar cheese	115 kcal
½ pint/10fl.oz. semi-skim milk	125 kcal
1 chocolate digestive biscuit	85 kcal
½ pint/10fl.oz. beer (bitter)	100 kcal
5fl.oz. dry white wine	95 kcal

Fibre
Daily requirement

adults and children	30 grams

Sources

1 orange	5.4 grams
1 medium baked potato	5.2 grams
1 slice wholewheat bread	2.7 grams
2 slices wholewheat crispbread	2.6 grams
1oz./25g bran flakes + 4fl.oz./ ½ cup semi-skim milk	2.5 grams

Calcium
Daily requirement

adults	500mg
teenagers and pregnant women	1,200mg

Sources

3oz./80g boiled spinach	500mg
8fl.oz./1 cup milk	300mg
1oz./25g cheese	250mg
1oz./25g cereal + 4fl.oz./ ½ cup semi-skim milk	160mg
1 tablespoon non-fat dried milk	52mg

Copper
Daily requirement

adults and children	2mg

Sources

6oz./160g ox liver	4.75mg
8fl.oz./1 cup whole milk	0.09mg

Iron
Daily requirement

adults and children	12mg

Sources

1oz./25g cereal + 4fl.oz./ ½ cup semi-skim milk	2.1mg

Potassium
Daily requirement

adults and children	2–3 grams

Sources

1oz./25g cornflakes + 4fl.oz./ ½ cup semi-skim milk	200mg
1oz./25g oatmeal	111mg
8fl.oz./1 cup whole milk	340mg

Sodium
Daily requirement

adults and children	1–3 grams

Sources

1 teaspoon salt	2.3 grams
1oz./25g cornflakes + 4fl.oz./ ½ cup semi-skim milk	400mg
1oz./25g oatmeal	10mg
7oz./200g baked beans	1 gram

Zinc
Daily requirement

adults and children	10mg

Sources

6oz./160g ox liver	7.2mg
1oz./25g cheese	1.1mg
8fl.oz./1 cup milk	0.93mg

Index

and risk factors, 13–14, 57
and saturated fat, 44–5, 62
and stress, 14
and sugar, 43, 61
and thromboxane, 48
and triglycerides, 14
and unsaturated fats, 48
and vegetarians, 71
and vitamin B$_6$, 69
and vitamin C, 47
and vitamin E, 69
Cerebrovascular disease (stroke), 15, 17, 25, 43
Cholestyramine, 52
Chromium, 70
Chylomicrons, 39–40
Cigarette smoking, 13, 17, 22, 72
Copper, 70
Coronary heart disease *see* Cardiovascular disease

Diabetes, 11, 14, 43, 57

Eicosapentaenoic acid (EPA), 50–51, 66
Endocrine glands, 31
Excretion of cholesterol, 27, 34, 40, 46
Exercise, 14, 22, 57, 58, 72

Fibre, 52, 53, 56, 59–61, 71, 72

Gall stones, 27, 32
Garlic, 71

HDL (High Density Lipoproteins), 21–7, 39, 50, 69, 71, 72
Heart attack, 15, 19, 21, 23, 45, 52, 79
Heart disease *see* Cardiovascular disease
Heredity, 14
Hormones, 9, 31, 39
Hypercholesterolaemia, 23
Hypertension, 11, 13, 16, 17, 57, 58, 68

LDL (Low Density Lipoproteins), 21, 22, 39, 40, 45, 50, 58, 69
Linoleic acid, 46, 48
Linolenic acid, 46, 48
Lipoproteins, 19–22, 38–40, 57, 58
  chylomicrons, 39, 40
  high density *see* HDL
  low density *see* LDL
  very low density *see* VLDL
Liver, 34–5, 39, 40, 45
Lymph fluid, 38

Magnesium, 70
Malnutrition, 62
Medications, 26–7
Monosaturated fats, 41

Niacin, 69

Obesity, 14, 22, 43, 57, 62
Oleic acid, 46
Oral contraceptives, 22

Phospholipids, 20
Platelets, 45, 47–51, 69, 71